START ANY BUSINESS

LET'S GET GOING!

Ian Moncrief-Scott

Information Management Solutions Limited

ISLE OF MAN

A CIP catalogue record for this book is available from the British Library

Published by Information Management Solutions Limited, 17 Howe Road, Onchan, Isle of Man, IM3 2BB.

Printed & Bound by IngramSpark

Book Layout © 2017 BookDesignTemplates.com

Cover design by Tanja Prokop of BookDesignTemplates.com

Superhero Peg Image: Besjunior/Shutterstock.com

START ANY BUSINESS (LET'S GET GOING) Ian Moncrief-Scott -- 1st ed.
ISBN 9781903467008

To the many aspiring entrepreneurs, their families, my colleagues and friends, who have trusted me.

CONTENTS

GREAT IDEA OR WANT TO WORK FOR YOURSELF?.............. 1

WHAT IS YOUR PLAN?.. 3

    PERSONAL STRENGTHS & WEAKNESSES 4

    BUSINESS STRENGTHS & WEAKNESSES 4

    WINDOW DRESSING.. 6

MARKET RESEARCH... 9

    INSIDE BEAUTY 9

SHORT-TERM CHANGES 11

    MY APPRENTICE STOLE MY BUSINESS 13

SOME NUMBERS 17

    PERSONAL SURVIVAL PLAN 17

    SETTING UP COSTS 17

    OTHER INITIAL OPERATING COSTS................................... 18

    BUDGETING & BREAK-EVEN POINT 18

FUNDING & SUPPORT 19

LEGAL STRUCTURES 21

PREMISES OR WORKING FROM HOME................................. 25

THE BUSINESS PLAN.. 27

    GRASS CUTTING TO TREE TRIMMING 28

MARKETING.. 31

    CUSTOMERS.. 32

    OPPORTUNITY LOST 33

    COMPETITION... 35

    SERVICE OR PRODUCT COMPARISON............................... 36

PROMOTION & SELLING 37

    WEBSITE 39

QUOTATIONS, ESTIMATES, PRICE LISTS & INVOICES..........41
    NUNS' BONES 43
    WHEN IS A SHADE NOT A SHADE? 47
PRICING & TACTICS 49
    SHOE STORY 50
BOOK & RECORD KEEPING 51
    PROFIT AND LOSS 53
    DEPRECIATION & CAPITAL ALLOWANCES..........53
    INCOME TAX & NATIONAL INSURANCE..............54
    VALUE ADDED TAX (VAT) 54
INTRODUCTION TO CASHFLOW..................................57
FINAL WORDS 59
    SWOT..61
    LIFE CHANGING EXPERIENCES............................62
    PERSONAL SURVIVAL PLAN................................63
    COMPETITOR COMPARISON 64
    INVOICE TEMPLATE...65
    CASHFLOW EXAMPLE 66
    CHECKLISTS...67
    BUSINESS PLAN 69
OTHER BOOKS BY THE AUTHOR 85
FORTHCOMING BOOKS BY THE AUTHOR 87

LET'S GET GOING!

CHAPTER ONE

GREAT IDEA OR WANT TO WORK FOR YOURSELF?

Most of the books that I have read start with forming a company, VAT registration, book-keeping or even getting an accountant before you do anything.

I have found that starting a business needs to go much further back than that.

This book will show you those vital steps.

It is much more important to know what running a business will mean to your family, your friends and, crucially, yourself.

Running a business, particularly as a sole-trader, is not for everybody.

This book will help you evaluate this before you need to worry about an accountant, book-keeper, obtaining premises or spending money.

In the early stages, they would be the last things on my mind.

Circumstances may have pushed many people into self-employment. For others, it is a choice or career step. The principles that I will show you apply in the same way.

Is it right for you or should you focus on getting another job in the same sector or changing to another type of employment?

These chapters will give you the tools to make an informed decision.

They will look at setting up costs, sources of funds, legal structures and putting together a basic business plan.

The next chapters will investigate marketing, target market, promotion to customers, competition, pricing, sales and the difference and pitfalls of quotations & estimates.

Finally, we will look very briefly into aspects of book-keeping, profit & loss, income tax, national insurance, VAT and cashflow, as they are amply covered elsewhere.

CHAPTER TWO

WHAT IS YOUR PLAN?

It could be an invention but most likely, it will involve a change from employment into self-employment.

What is it you plan to do?

Please write your idea down. Putting something on the computer or paper will help you define clearly what it is you would like to happen and what you don't want to occur.

What is the biggest challenge you think you are going to face? For most people, it is never having run a business before. You could be worried about pricing, asking people for money or raising cash.

Again, please write it down.

Why do you think self-employment is right for you? You know the next step already... write it down!

OK, now that we are working together, let's look at the basics.

PERSONAL STRENGTHS & WEAKNESSES

Take a few minutes to list your personal strengths.

These could be skills, knowledge, experience, qualifications or sources of support. You might need a few extra sheets of paper for this!!

Now take a few more minutes to write down your weaknesses.

For example, do you like asking people for money?

This is a vitally important part of being in business. If you don't like asking, how are you going to solve or get around this need?

People do business with other people and talking to other people is essential in business.

So, do we need any training? Should we delegate or avoid it? Are we going to have to recruit internally or externally before we launch?

BUSINESS STRENGTHS & WEAKNESSES

Let's now do the same for a business.

For a business to be successful, what do you think its key strengths should be?

Early suggestions from new entrepreneurs are usually soft-skill based, such as flexibility, reliability or approachability.

A higher business focus would be securing and retaining customers, identifying and dealing with the competition, ensuring a profit, correct location, effective pricing and access to capital.

If we now look at business weaknesses, let's assume the opposite of the points made in business strengths apply.

What we are looking for are the specific reasons why businesses fail.

Most start-ups and expanders fail due to cashflow.

It does not reflect a lack of commitment or enthusiasm or even a full order book. Running out of cash by expanding too quickly, not having fast access to working capital, getting slow payers and bad debt are frequently the causes.

Under-pricing is another reason.

Many start-ups think they have to be cheaper than the competition and, consequently, fail to cover overheads or appear inferior.

Location, if relying on passing trade, can become an issue.

Finally, not conducting adequate market research, particularly bearing in mind your catchment area, demographics and market size, could be another reason for failure.

Here is an example of how things can go wrong:

WINDOW DRESSING

I used to pick my wife up from work and take her home. Almost invariably, we got stuck at the village traffic lights controlled by so-called artificial intelligence.

They were neither artificial nor intelligent as they seemed to pounce at every opportunity. While waiting for the change to green, Tina, my wife, often looked across me from the passenger seat towards a large select clothes shop on the other side of the road.

She would say, "They have a nice red dress in the window. I'll go and try that on."

Having been "trained" over many the years to give the "right" answer, I would respond, "You have always looked good in red."

The lights would change and then we would head home.

A few days later, we would get stuck again. This time my wife might say, "Look, Ian, there is a very nice blue dress next to the red dress."

Without hesitation, I gave the "correct" answer, "You always look great in blue, why don't you buy them both.

It went on for years!

Though it had a massive display front, Tina never walked the mile from work to the shop or took holiday time to go. There was no parking nearby. There were yellow no-parking lines on both sides of the road, which was busy and narrow.

Crucially, the shop was never open before or after regular work hours or at the weekend.

As such, it was an excellent advertising hoarding but almost useless as a retail sales venue. It closed shortly afterwards.

Sometimes people take me to one side and say things like you know how hard it to find suitable, cheap premises. Often, their voice goes hushed, "Well, I got this great shop on Obscure Street and its only £50 per week all in.

I think to myself, I have lived here for many, many years and have never come across that place. "So where is it exactly," I enquire.

"You know the bus station, it's behind there down an alley at the back of the pubs, just beyond the wheelie bins," comes the excited response.

"Tell me, are you relying on passing trade, going to sell online or make something there," I ask.

"Passing trade is vital. I am relying on that!"

"Well, it sounds to me that there will be plenty on a Friday and Saturday night when you are closed but the rest of the time, I could see most people steering well clear of that location!

In the previous paragraphs, we have learned one of the basic business tools called "SWOT." We have looked at Strengths and Weaknesses in some detail and the Opportunities we have identified by our basic market research.

However, that leaves the "T" in SWOT.

Unlike Weaknesses, Threats are not usually something that we can influence but we do have to be very mindful of them.

Threats might include economic conditions, reputational risk, new or emerging competition, regulation or high travel costs.

You can use SWOT in many aspects, including yourself, customers and competition. An example is in Appendix 1.

CHAPTER THREE

MARKET RESEARCH

Before you commit to anything, it will help to carry out initial market research to assess demand and see if being in business is right for you. Let me give you a couple of personal experiences.

INSIDE BEAUTY

There have been a few very different businesses attending my training courses but the principles of a start-up are very much the same for almost everyone. I recall two individuals wishing to start-up as colonic irrigators.

The first lady I met was the butt of much of my own and the group's humour. To be honest, I was not looking forward to shaking her hands when I awarded a Certificate of Attendance.

She took the friendly jibes with excellent humour. However, she returned the favour fully on the second part of the course when she brought in the largest nozzle from her kit and offered free sessions for me and a couple of others. I promptly declined with thanks and made a hasty exit.

The other start-up decided that she was going to go on the treatment training course before she spent any more money. It proved to be the right decision as she became the guinea pig for treatment during training and realised it was not for her.

CHAPTER FOUR

SHORT-TERM CHANGES

Once we embark on this new adventure, particularly in the short term, our lives are going to change, not always for the better.

Let us have a look at some potential areas of change and how this might affect us positively and, in some cases, negatively.

Taking control is often given as the main reason many people want to start their own business. The downside of this is responsibility. There is no-one else to blame. You cannot blame that boss for changing his or her mind. You are now the only person responsible for making things happen, for correcting faults and for managing your business.

Independence is another reason given for setting off on your own.

However, one opposite consequence could now be your inability to delegate. There is no-one else unless you employ someone or pay for work to be done.

It inevitably leads to the need for multi-tasking... becoming a jack of all trades and, vitally, a master of most!

Frequently, you will find that multi-tasking requires you to become the record administrator, book-keeper, stock controller, buyer, seller, maker, deliverer and manager.

These roles often lead to long hours, making it the most bemoaned part of starting a new business.

Unfortunately, long hours and pressure of start-up unknowns can lead to stress and anxiety.

In some circumstances, it can lead to illness. How will you manage to run your business if you are unwell or, worse still, injure yourself?

Let's imagine you like playing football and you break your leg. You are a window cleaner. How are you going to climb ladders, let alone find enough bungalows on which to work?

People often count on their insurance cover but this can be slow to pay out if it meets claims at all.

Perhaps, you can rely on or friends and family? Are you able to pre-pare them to step in should there be an emergency?

Friends can be helpful. You may have test marketed your business using friends' feedback and, even given special pricing arrangements, sometimes known as "mates" rates. Do you still need to do this or perhaps you can exchange their skills for yours?

Speaking of family, especially if you are working from home. How are you going to deal with this aspect? Will you all be using the same computer? What about security & data protection? Do you need to think about Internet access and broadband restrictions?

If you are going to have clients visiting you at home, how will you separate your business life from your private one? Will you need a separate entrance or quiet/confidential zone?

We will cover working from home separately later.

What about going on holiday? Leaving aside whether you can now afford them, will you be restricted when you can take them? Will your partner have to take the children away on their own?

What will happen to your clients and customers when you are away? Will friends and family or staff run the business for you? Can you just put a sign up on the door saying "had an outstanding year, gone to St Lucia, see you in a month!"?

Will you need a van instead of a family car? Is it going to be liveried to help you market your venture?

Perhaps, you had a valuable employee pension? How are you going to fund that in the future?

MY APPRENTICE STOLE MY BUSINESS

An attendee on one of the first training courses explained why he was there.

"I went on holiday and that's why I have come on your course," he kept repeating.

I enquired further. "Well, it was my fault because I went on holiday!" came the exclamation.

"Sorry, I don't see the connection," I remarked.

"Well, I had not had a holiday for seven years while I was building my business and now, I am on your training course," he pursued his theme.

"Sorry, I am not joining up the dots here," I replied. *"Could you start at the beginning to help me."*

"I had not taken a day off for seven years and decided to take one long break in Spain for six weeks with my family... and that's why I am on your course," he continued.

"So, you went on holiday. What happened next?" I said.

"Well, I decided to have a complete break and did not take my phone or laptop," he went on.

"Right," I added, *"but I still don't see where you are going with this?"*

"Well, you see, I had taken this youngster on as an apprentice when I first started, trained him and the customers loved him, so that's why I am on your course," he clarified.

We were getting somewhere now, what a responsible man, I thought but I still could not make the connection.

Fortunately, he was now in full flight. "Well, I needed someone to look after the business while I was away as I could not just close it temporarily as it ran 24/7," he progressed. *"So, I left it in the hands of the apprentice and now I needed to come on your course."*

The theme had returned but there was now forward motion. "Aha!" I uttered the pennies beginning to drop. "It did not take him long to wreck it for you then."

"Wreck it, wreck it," he retorted, *"He did not wreck it. Once I had stepped on the plane, he contacted all my customers. He told them that I had beaten my wife, gone on the run, embezzled company funds, owed thousands of pounds and was hiding in Spain forever!"*

He explained further, "The coup de grâce was that the poor apprentice now had to start on his own to feed his family with a brand-new business. He added that he would try to look after all my former customers seamlessly.

As a consequence, when I came back, relaxed, tanned and happy, my business was gone. No-one would believe a word I said and I have come on your training course to learn how to run a business properly!"

Consequently, have you got a sound backup plan if you need someone to look after your business for holidays, buying trips or illness?

Suggestions for areas you may wish to consider are in Appendix 2.

CHAPTER FIVE

SOME NUMBERS

PERSONAL SURVIVAL PLAN

Now might be a good time to review your personal expenditure and household budgets to establish how much net income you will need to sustain yourself once you start your enterprise.

Examining family circumstances in this way will help you understand any future lifestyle changes that might be necessary.

There is a template to help assess your circumstances in Appendix 3.

SETTING UP COSTS

Now let us try to calculate the minimum amount of money that you will need to open for business.

Depending on the nature of your new venture, this might encompass expense areas, such as rent, stock, IT, vehicle, equipment, training, accreditation insurance, legal and company fees, etc.

OTHER INITIAL OPERATING COSTS

The next stage is to try to establish the minimum amount of money needed to operate your start-up for the next 3-6 months while you are building your income. Costs could include telephone, fuel, employees' wages, etc.

BUDGETING & BREAK-EVEN POINT

It is well worth knowing the point at which you expect to breakeven. To do this, you can either express it by the number of sales needed or the date by which your sales income has exceeded your operating costs.

It is a good idea to ignore pre-start expenses and capital expenditure as this will distort the figures. What we want to identify is the point at which the business will trade positively.

CHAPTER SIX

FUNDING & SUPPORT

How are you going to fund your new business? For example, do you have savings, loans or friends & family that might provide gifts and loans?

These loans might require security or silent/active participation in your venture. Will they be interest-bearing or interest-free and when will they have to be repaid?

You might wish to consider external sources, like banks for overdrafts or loans, crowdfunding, investors or so-called business angels.

How are you going to approach them? Most will require a business plan, security and many may want to take equity in your venture or have a profit share.

Take great care in the use of credit cards or placing your home and other assets at risk for security and guarantee purposes. It is worth exploring all alternatives and critically examining your business plan before making this highly risky commitment.

At this stage, it is well worth exploring to see if there is any support or assistance available to you to start and develop your business.

It could be in the form of local government and agency grants, loans, training, advice or mentoring. These organisations may also be able to provide free information on matters, such as data protection, health & safety, regulatory requirements, licences, inspections and approvals.

It might be positive to contact your local Chambers of Commerce, trade bodies, etc. Options might include The Prince's Trust and Shell Live Wire.

Business Angels or crowdfunding might be something to consider but be careful sharing ideas and releasing equity or control.

Professional advisors, such as solicitors, accountants and architects might be helpful. However, you should be sure of the cost and what you are getting for your money.

Other business owners, friends or family could prove useful.

Now might be an excellent time to consider opening a bank account if you have not already got one.

They can take some time to open because of due diligence checks.

It is always a good idea to have a different bank account for your business so that personal expenditure does not get mixed up with your business transactions.

If you are not trading in your name, it is highly likely that the bank will require sight of documents. These could include your business plan, name certificate and company particulars.

CHAPTER SEVEN

LEGAL STRUCTURES

OK, so we are going to go ahead and launch our business, what are the next steps?

There are a few choices. The simplest is to become self-employed as a sole trader, which in most jurisdictions just involves informing the tax authorities of your decision. Most are content to let you continue in full or part-time employment as well if you wish.

Try to get into the habit of calling money you withdraw from the business "drawings" and not wages. You are actually drawing profit in advance and the funds may well be liable for potential Income Tax and National Insurance charges.

You can trade in your name.

However, a separate business name is usually straightforward. Some authorities require you to register the name and show your name on letterheads, quotations and estimates, etc. You would typically place these at the foot of the page.

Usually, you do not have to disclose details of your business finances to anyone other than the tax authorities nor have to produce formal accounts. However, you still have to pay Income Tax and National Insurance at the self-employed rates.

By trading in your name or name of your choice, you are the official legal entity.

If you get into financial difficulties or become insolvent, creditors will look directly to you for any debts. It could mean that your home or other assets are potentially at risk.

Some people prefer to work with others. There could be an advantage as one of you might be good at selling; the other party could be good at administration.

It is always a good idea to draw up a partnership agreement detailing who is responsible for different aspects and how you will treat assets and remuneration. Importantly, you may want to specify what happens if one of you decides not to continue with the business.

The obligations are similar to a sole-trader in that no formal accounts are usually required and you only need to inform the tax office.

Vitally though, partnerships are jointly and severally liable for the debts of each partner personally and can be risky if they unravel.

You can mitigate potential issues by using structures, such as "limited liability partnerships" or "partnerships limited by guarantee." With these arrangements, a cap is placed on the amount at risk, provided there is no illegal activity taking place.

The main alternative to being a sole-trader or partnership is a limited company.

These separate you from the business by creating an independent legal entity, which affords better protection if issues develop. Often, these can happen through no fault of your own, such as getting a bad debt or slow payer.

Forming a limited company typically requires at least one director. Many jurisdictions require two. A minimum of one shareholder is needed but more can be involved.

You will need to establish Memorandum and Articles of Association, which set out the rules of corporate conduct. Local start-up hubs, chambers of commerce and online help sources can often provide suitable templates.

Frequently, there is a small application fee. Once an application is approved, you should receive a Certificate of Incorporation, which will show the date and company number. The latter should appear on invoices, letterheads and correspondence, etc.

On the anniversary of incorporation (i.e., the forming of a company), an annual return to the company registry is required. Depending on the jurisdiction, a copy of the company's yearly accounts might also need to be submitted, together with details of beneficial ownership. Forms will be available from the registry.

Any changes to directors, addresses, etc., between annual returns, are usually required to be notified to the registry on the appropriate form, accompanied by the fee.

Dealing with the requirements of the company administration, such as holding board and shareholder meetings, maintaining minute records are currently beyond the scope of this book. You may be able to get help from the parties that may have produced the initial documents.

In many jurisdictions, there is no requirement for an independent audit if turnover falls below a specific level. However, an investor or lender may require one as a condition of supporting you.

An advantage of a limited company is the ability of the shareholders to take a dividend. Unlike employee wages and drawings, these do not attract National Insurance charges in many jurisdictions.

CHAPTER EIGHT

PREMISES OR WORKING FROM HOME

Working from home may require planning permission. It may not be forthcoming if you are going to make noise or create nuisance like smells, parking or attracting vermin. You might find that regulations, such as food-hygiene, may also apply.

If you expect to allow clients to visit you, there may be safety, access or timing considerations.

Landlords, mortgage providers and insurers should be informed by a simple recorded letter. Try to word it so you are notifying them of a change but not inviting an automatic price or premium increase. Some landlords will be reluctant to have their address used in case of potential, future bad debt blacklisting.

If you are going to use independent premises, it is essential to check planning requirements and any other nearby planning applications to evaluate impact.

Other considerations are leases. Are they fully repairable and must premises be left as found?

Take photographs of any damage or maintenance issues before you sign the lease or, immediately, should any problems arise later.

Lease conditions could include sub-letting limitations and restrictions on other types of businesses at the premises. They may also cover rent change criteria, end of term conditions, possible purchase arrangements, official notices and tenant or other occupant behaviour.

If the change of use is required, it is a good idea to seek a letter of comfort from planners and try to obtain an agreement in principle with the landlord. He can walk away before the contract is signed and it can be beneficial not to commence any work ahead of documentation completion.

If working from home, there could be income tax allowances on rent, power and insurance costs.

It might be a good idea to create family rules and boundaries, such as telephone and computer use, background noise, availability, etc.

CHAPTER NINE

THE BUSINESS PLAN

We could now move forward to assessing the feasibility of our idea. It could be in the form of a simple study or the preparation of an initial business plan.

Why would this help?

Simply writing it down is better than it is just in your head.

It will help you remember the many assumptions you will have to make.

Documenting it can provide you with proof of concept and record or evaluate any third-party interests.

Overall, it will help you ensure you miss as little as possible.

A business plan will enable you to make historical comparisons of assumptions and actuals. It will give you the basis to review changes and support your implementation and processes.

A sample business plan and a checklist are in Appendix 7 & 8

GRASS CUTTING TO TREE TRIMMING

Let's imagine we are going to set up as a gardener, or not so much a gardener, more as a grass cutter.

First of all, let's establish what exactly we are going to do and describe it. I am going to cut grass in East town. Note, I am deliberately targeting East town because lots of elderly folks live there in traditional houses. They have medium to large lawns that they are unable or unwilling to maintain themselves. I am not going to target West town, as it is mainly full of offices, flats and concrete.

I reckon I can cut six lawns a day. That would leave one day per week free because of rain to carry out maintenance and paperwork (other than invoicing, which I am going to keep on top of and do daily).

What am I going to charge? I have heard that most cutters charge about £25.00 per hour for the service. I'll match that price and armed with that information I can now draft my sales forecast.

So, what about the competition? There are plenty of vans about, some of which have names and contact details on them. I'll observe those for a few weeks and then try to establish my competitive edge, sometimes known as my USP (Unique Selling Point/Proposition).

I need to think about marketing and getting my name out there. Word of mouth is potent here and a few business cards should do the trick. I may have to do a little bit of leaflet dropping and adverts in Post Offices and supermarkets to get me started. More thought about this is needed.

I will have my name and contact details on my van together with a statement of what I do and, ideally, my USP!

In East town, cats and gulls abound and there is a real shortage of small birds. My target audience clearly cares about cats.

Consequently, one of my USPs will be to make sure I don't run over any while I am cutting the grass. That would really upset my customers if I turned their lawn from green to red!

Cats are used to noisy lawnmowers but what about deaf cats that like hiding in the long grass? They could come to harm and that could be a real risk and threat to my business. Public Liability insurance and my training/qualifications would be useless in preventing a disaster!

I know how to overcome this. I will have some flashing lights on my mower. That will do the trick. If they cannot hear the blades, they will see the flashing lights and scarper pronto!

What about blind cats, I hear you say? Well, if they are let out or escape, that could be an issue. Perhaps, I had better have some additional background noise in case they have become over-casual to the sound of a lawnmower or strimmer? Some high-pitched bells will do the trick here.

When putting the finishing touches to my sales forecast, I note that grass does not grow in the winter. There will be no income and I don't think I can save enough to carry me over the period. What else can I do? What do other grass cutters do?

End of year gales might bring down some trees. Dealing with them is specialist work and usually handed to more experienced firms.

However, gardens usually have bushes that need sprucing up, winter or early spring trimming or the cleaning of paths that have gathered moss. I will focus on that.

The approach is key to this new development. I could just bowl into a customer and say that tree branch looks dangerous. It could kill someone. It will cost you £200 to have it cut and then you will have to pay extra for it to be chipped or taken away.

On the other hand, I am easy to do business with and have built up a friendly, reliable and trusting relationship with my new customer over the summer.

I would be better saying, "I have been carefully watching your garden while cutting the grass and have noticed a broken tree branch.

It would be a good idea to get that looked at, it should only cost less than £200 and there would be a couple of added benefits. The sun would then help the grass stay greener and reduce moss on your paths to avoid the cost of frequent cleaning and the risk of slipping.

You could even put a small seat in that area and watch the sun going down with a gin and tonic.

I could do it for you if you liked and take the wood away for you for nothing." (The latter would give me some nice, dry, free of charge logs for my winter burner).

CHAPTER TEN

MARKETING

OK, let's move on now to the factors we should consider as part of our market research.

Do we have a name for our new venture? If we are going to use a name other than exactly our name, we may well have to register it with the local company registry. The authority will ensure it has not allocated the name already or that it breaches regulations covering offensive names and protected ones. The latter could include banks and other financial institutions.

Remember that having a domain name does not protect you from someone registering the same or similar name with an official registry. It also does not comply with official company name registration.

Some people prefer a catchy name, others one which describes what they are doing. For example, in the first case, it could be "eureka." In the second case, it could be "John Smith Plumber." It might be more expensive to raise awareness of what "eureka" is all about. Whereas John Smith Plumber, with his contact details, driving past in his van, speaks for itself.

It would now be worth looking in more detail at the most critical areas of pre-business launch, customers, promotion and competitors.

CUSTOMERS

What do you need to know about your customers?

You may wish to build a demographic profile. However, there are other aspects to consider.

Does the customer need your product or service? Can they pay and what are their price expectations?

Is the customer a buyer or a user? For instance, a buyer might be more interested in price and availability. Performance and reliability might be ranked more significantly by a user.

Having done the hard bit to gain a customer or gain interest, can you sell them anything else? The chances are they will have researched the first product or service but may not have researched other products or services. It may give you sales-margin opportunities and extra sales turnover, with the bonus of added customer satisfaction.

For example, someone wishes to purchase a new fishing rod, can you sell them some bait, a net, waders or a reel?

Is the customer likely to be a repeat customer? If so, will they expect to be remembered? Do you wish to take into account future sales and offer a loyalty discount?

Hairdressers and beauty therapists are usually very good with repeat customers, by asking questions about holidays, interests, dislikes so that they can build trust and rapport.

Where are your customers based? Will you have to travel to them? Will they expect a home visit?

Recognising the decision-maker is an essential aspect and may not be obvious. A purchasing department may not be involved and the real choice could rest in the hands of a shop-floor official, receptionist or goods receiving supervisor.

Household purchasing is the same. Who holds the purse strings? Do brand names and reputations overarch prices?

OPPORTUNITY LOST

My wife, Tina and I visit a local builders' merchant. It is an exciting place because the double doors open as you approach them. A young man, like one in weather or cuckoo clock, swings out to greet us. He is well-dressed in a suit and tie with a waistcoat. Gareth Southgate probably dressed him!

"Good morning Sir. Welcome to our store," comes the cheery greeting. "That's a nice Porsche you have, Sir, what year is it?"

"Oh, it's only an old one," I say, "1988."

"Have you had it long?" follows the initial enquiry.

"Thirteen years," I add.

"You look very tanned and healthy, have you been away?" the conversation continues.

"Yes, we've just got back from two weeks in the Canaries," I respond, seeing my wife itching to enter the store.

I like this young man and he seems genuinely interested in me.

"Are you going to watch the match this afternoon?" comes the next question.

"Got my seat booked in front of the TV. The sooner, the better I escape from here," I chuckle.

Meanwhile, Tina has got bored with standing by and watching the conversation. Since the subject has now moved to football, she politely sidesteps the nice young man to get into the store.

We move onto politics. "Do you think there will be an election this year?" he asks.

"Hopefully," I remark, "This lot couldn't manage a drinking party in a brewery, let alone run a country."

I hear kitchen doors being opened and closed firmly. Goodness knows what is happening to the white goods' doors.

"So, what do you make of the weather this year?" he enquires.

"Sick of the rain and the wind, can't wait to get away again," I respond. We are getting to become quite good friends now. He understands me and knows all the right buttons to push.

My wife is exasperated and I can hear the sound of tiles hitting the marble floor.

Perhaps, the young man will venture in to see what is causing all the commotion?

He stays straight in my face. A sale is evaporating behind him.

I am not the decision-maker.

My wife has decided that we are going to have a new kitchen, what units we are going to have, when fitting will happen, the price and how I am going to pay for it.

I am only the driver... she is the decision-maker and the person on whom the nice, young man should have focussed his efforts.

COMPETITION

What do you need to know about your competitors?

We can learn a lot from our competitors. How they do things, have they followed industry trends, kept pace with technology, or made any public mistakes?

Do you have a main competitor that perhaps controls the market or can influence sources of supply in the marketplace?

Is this competitor likely to take a hostile or benign approach to you?

What do your competitors offer? Do they have a more extensive range? How do they promote themselves to reach their customers? Do they have a competitive edge other than already supplying the market and being established?

A crucial step would be to try to see why they appeal to customers.

So, how are you going to deal with your competition? There may be circumstances when you can feed off them should they be unable to satisfy demand and need backup capacity.

You might have to co-operate with your competition if required by project contract terms.

The competition might provide a helpful solution if you are unable to meet demand yourself because of peaks, troughs, holidays or under mutual referral arrangements.

Some of the more hostile (and often illegal) ways of dealing with competitors should be best left aside. Passive methods offering ethical and sustainable solutions far outweigh orchestrating bad social media reviews, making false bookings or maliciously reporting competitors to the authorities.

Positive steps could be pricing, quality, promotion methods, staff training, location, opening hours and after-sales service.

SERVICE OR PRODUCT COMPARISON

It will be useful if you can compare yourself to your competitors to try to establish your main selling points. There is a template offering a helpful start with the areas you may wish to consider in Appendix 4.

CHAPTER ELEVEN

PROMOTION & SELLING

How do you want to be seen by your potential customers? What are the messages you are going to give them and how are you going to reach them?

There are many promotional choices. You could choose from business cards, directories, flyers, giveaways, media advertising, t-shirts, signage, billboards and mugs. Events and locations could include grand openings, themed or special events and markets.

Promotion initiatives, often called marketing campaigns, can waste a great deal of money. There are crucial steps you can take to avoid this.

You have identified your target audience. Does the promoter reach your target audience? Ask them. If it does not, walk away, as it will be a waste of your money to proceed and you are likely to get no leads, let alone sales.

Try to establish that by spending money on promotion, how many new sales are likely to be produced. How much money will you make after taking into consideration the costs involved? It is called cost-benefit analysis.

If you engage a copyrighter, photographer or designer, who owns the copyright? There is a presumption that it vests with the creator and not the person paying for the work.

Consequently, it is a good idea to buy the copyright as part of your purchase, especially if you may want to use the work in another way, for example, in an advertisement. It is usually free to obtain it at this stage but can be expensive or cause delays later.

Testimonials and assurances of potential success can be beneficial. It can prove fruitful to ignore rate cards in favour of negotiating prices and seeking performance guarantees.

There are many free and cheap sources of promotion. Word of mouth, referrals, business cards and social media can prove constructive. Fairs, festivals, community groups, and markets can all be useful. They are usually inexpensive sources too.

Finally, cold calls offering wall planners, directories and calendars are best disregarded, especially those purporting to support a charity. Any harassment is a matter for the Police and Trading Standards.

When it comes to selling, keep it simple. Be accessible, turn up when promised or at least let the customer know of any unforeseen delays. Return phone calls. Try to avoid unnecessary conflict.

Highlight the benefits of your service or product and not just rely on their features.

Make notes of client preferences and personal details in the case of repeat customers to build empathy and develop relationships.

Overall, help customers to do business with you with ease!

WEBSITE

Some people believe that a website or social media page is essential.

Again, it is a potential promotion tool. What will it cost in time and money to acquire one and then keep it up to date? A cost-benefit analysis will help here, especially when it comes to only reaching your target audience. You don't want it to become a vanity publication that no-one else will see.

Who will provide research, content and photographs? Is it a referral site or is search engine success needed? Who will update the site? Can you update it yourself using office tools like Excel or Word?

As with any purchase, take up references, obtain two or three quotes and make your desired outcomes written conditions of purchase.

Three final steps are to put a few relevant (to you) search terms into a web search engine. See which sites appear.

Check their strengths to make comparisons with your designer. Also, put appropriate search terms (not their name) into a web engine to see if your proposed designer appears in the first pages. If they cannot achieve this for themselves, how can they do it for you?

Take care of budget control when using online advertising as the costs can spiral without real benefit.

Please ensure that the domain name ownership is registered to you and not any third party. It could avoid being held to "ransom" during the renewal process or the transfer of ownership to you.

CHAPTER TWELVE

QUOTATIONS, ESTIMATES, PRICE LISTS & INVOICES

There are several similarities between the documents that can help avoid later conflict.

Putting phrases like "valid until" or "offer ends on," etc., have the benefit of encouraging the potential customer to act early. They can avoid misunderstandings that the offer is open-ended.

If you are VAT registered, your pricing documents should include VAT and you should clearly state this. If your customers are VAT registered, they may prefer a VAT exclusive price and the VAT rate shown separately.

Whereas, if they are private individuals or not VAT registered, they may prefer you to give the actual payment required.

It is beneficial to consider any special legal conditions that might exist in some jurisdictions. For example, "ROMALPA," which can mean that title in the goods does not pass to the other party unless specific stipulations, e.g., payment are met.

When it comes to terms and timing of payment, this is a negotiation similar to the price. Many individuals and companies believe they have an automatic right to pay in 30 days, against a monthly statement or when directors are available to sanction payments or transfers.

Try to make sure there is clarity at the offer and acceptance point. It can avoid you gifting additional credit facilities at your expense and increasing the risk to your cashflow.

Some people believe that early payment discounts may encourage their customers to pay more promptly.

You may well find that using the phrase, "Invoices will attract interest at x% above XYZ Bank's minimum lending rate and title in the goods do not pass until payment is received in full," can have an effective bearing on payment outcomes.

It is a bit like having a burglar alarm. A customer might find it better to abuse a neighbouring property (supplier) rather than you. You have given the impression of being professional, especially if you have asked around, checked their payment reputation and taken up trade references as well.

Obtaining prepayments for third-party bookings or materials needed can significantly reduce your exposure to potential bad debts.

Agreed stage payments are a similar helpful tool.

It can be helpful to "test" the customer at this stage. Bad payers, when materials are delivered on-site or samples are submitted, are likely to act the same when you complete the job.

Indeed, some people believe it is their right to renegotiate prices and discounts on completion when they have you over a barrel.

Unexpected quality and workmanship issues can suddenly emerge when payments become due.

Prepayments are preferable to deposits. It is presumed that they are part of your ongoing expenditure rather than held separately should the customer decide not to proceed to contract fulfilment. They also substantially improve cashflow.

What is most important is the use of written documents for sign-offs, offer and acceptance and, crucially, completion, as these will help you increase the chances of getting paid.

Relying on verbal understandings and agreements, which are difficult to prove, can be disastrous.

NUNS' BONES

One day the director told me to get the fireplace in the board room removed as people were always falling over the hearth.

I contacted an experienced local builder, who was familiar with the premises and the estate in general. The next day we met and I asked him for a written quotation, confirming the price, start and finish dates.

In his typical cheery voice, he said that the work would start next Monday and would be finished in two days, if not painted. He asked what I wanted to do with the fire-surround and he said he would give me £500 for it. I offered to have the tea on mid-morning.

On Monday he turned up on time and about 10.00 am my phone rang. The receptionist said the builder wants to meet urgently. I thought that would be the call for the tea.

Arriving in the board room, the builder was wringing his hands.... I immediately thought my tea was more needed than I had anticipated.

"Ian, we've got a problem, we have found bones behind the fireplace!"

"So" was my reply.

"Well, they could be a nun's bones!" came the response.

Unearthed nuns' bones were quite commonplace at the site, a former Nunnery dating back over 1000 years. Occasionally, though, it might have been the skeleton of a racehorse, as one of the previous owners was racing trainer.

Come off it mate, I said, it's going to be a crow or a heron.

"Can't take the risk. I'll have to report it. The Police and the local heritage trust will get involved and we'll have to find a clergyman to consecrate them. There'll be a cordon around the room for months!"

"Oh, well, if that's the case, so be it," I replied.

"That's so good of you, Ian, I thought you would kick-off."

"Not a problem, mate," I agreed.

"I am relieved," the builder sighed.

"So am I, you gave me a written, unconditional, fixed price and a set timetable. You are an experienced professional and there was no mention of any potential delay."

"That is kind of you to say," came his reply.

"Well, you should have made it clear that the prices and dates were conditional on not finding nuns' bones. We charge £400 per day for the rental of the room, five days a week and you think it will be over two months before it is next in use.

Do you want to take the invoice for the loss of income of £16,000 plus VAT with you today or shall I post it?"

Price lists can be useful, especially if you do not like asking people for money. "Here is my price list," can be a helpful phrase as discussions reach the money stage.

Now let's have a look at one of the main areas of potential conflict between you and your customer and how we can mitigate it or avoid it altogether.

Written estimates and quotations are crucial.

State your terms of business, including price, payment, guarantees, completion, stage dates and what is being done and not done.

If the customer needs to provide materials, photographs, copy, text or other information, especially if in a particular format or timescale, you should include it in the documentation.

Add any terms you feel might be relevant. For instance, you might want to mention currency exchange fluctuations or items subject to supplier price increases. VAT rates or alternative products you might use because of availability can also prove useful.

Let's now decide if we should provide a quotation or estimate.

Estimates in good faith are useful when there are unknowns. These could be having to work with the customer's third parties or following specific exploratory work. It will help you protect yourself better.

Quotations, on the other hand, should be more certain proposals. You can still add "subject to" but there is an expectation that a quotation is a firm price.

As a general rule, buyers and customers prefer a quotation, whereas suppliers may seek to issue an estimate.

The next aspect is the classic situation of "while you are here or while you are making it, can I just change or add ABC?"

It can be an opportunity but it can also turn into a minefield.

Try to make sure before you agree to modify or vary the contract that everybody understands the delay and extra charges which could emerge. Otherwise, with the best intentions, you go ahead and add the additional electrical socket, with all the hidden supporting cable only to encounter drama.

Such is likely to occur when you invoice the customer for the extra amount. You then receive the customary hands on hips response, "Had I known it was going to cost that much more, I would not have asked you to do it."

Now, much if not all, of the customer goodwill you have earned and, the countless cups of tea you have consumed, will count for nothing.

At best, you will have a disgruntled customer. At worst, the customer might dispute your bill through the courts.

Think carefully about giving price breakdowns. It is good practise to list all of the services and materials. If you price them individually, one of two things could happen.

The customer might say, "Oh, one of your competitors can do that part cheaper," or worse still, "I have seen that on an online auction site for half that price."

You may well now have to reduce your price, lose that element to a competitor or have to use a counterfeit item. If you use it, you have accepted responsibility for subsequent faults or quality claims.

WHEN IS A SHADE NOT A SHADE?

My wife had been on at me to get the front room re-painted. Quite simply, I had now run out of excuses, sorry, reasons, for not spending the money and the spare bed was being made up ready.

"I'd like it painted in "September Mist," please," she enthused, "You could ask that nice man, Fred, to do it."

"OK, I'll speak to him tomorrow but it could be months before he comes as he is so popular." "No problem," came the reply.

As promised, I agreed on a price for "September Mist," which looked remarkably like standard, trade magnolia but with a 400% price difference.

Months went by and, on cue, Fred and his men arrived and started work immediately without the need for a tea break or reading of the newspaper. A promising sign, I thought, as I left for the office.

Three days later I was sitting at my desk and my phone rang, "It's marvellous, we should have had this work done years ago, perfect job. I've told Fred you'll send a cheque tonight and there will be a generous tip!"

I have to say I was relieved. The spare bed did not beckon and now I could begin the stalling process for the new curtains, carpet and lighting that would inevitably come into play!

"You know what," Tina said, "I am so thrilled I am going to invite Madge round for a coffee this afternoon to show off a bit."

My heart sank, I cannot choose my wife's friends but Marge fell into a different category... some people called her very special!

Sure enough, Marge could not turn down the invitation to see the new opus magnum. Coffee in hand, she stalked the room. "Oh, look, they've missed a bit there and that cutting-in is not very clean. What was the colour again? "September Mist," it looks like "Autumn Dew" to me!" she oozed caustically.

"Did you check the label on the tins and were they open before they arrived? You know what these painters are like, they'll have swopped the proper paint for some cheap trade mix, you know."

Tina was devastated. Her new expert surveying friend had spotted a scam, "When Ian comes home, he can get onto that Fred fellow and tell him to come and put the job right, no tip for him!"

I strolled into the lounge, with an expectation of praise for my small part in a job well done. Instead, I got full bore, "You can ring that Fred fellow and tell him to put the job right and there'll be no tip for him! After recovering from the initial shock, I noticed a letterhead on the table. "What's this?" I said. "Oh, I just signed that when I thought he had done a great job and before Marge pointed out the many shortcomings."

"We have known Fred for many years and he has always been good. That paper you have signed is a satisfaction certificate, and you have also endorsed it with the words "great job, many thanks." I cannot go back to him now. I can ask him to redo it but we will have to pay again. In all the excitement had Marge forgotten to wear her specs, you know how myopic she is?"

"Maybe you're right and I overreacted. It was just having my donkey kicked over after all this time I have waited, maybe some new curtains would set it off?"

Disaster over but it did highlight the importance of getting things in writing and that a satisfaction or completion note can help avoid future problems.

CHAPTER THIRTEEN

PRICING & TACTICS

It is one of the most challenging areas for start-ups to assess. Close observation of competition is essential to potentially mirror existing market prices but offer something extra, such as "free" delivery or installation.

You can use a variety of techniques. For example, discounting can move particular stock quickly, reward customer loyalty, take account of seasonal factors or pass on supplier discounts.

Some terms you might be familiar with could be "Temporary Price Reduction" (TPR), "Buy One Get One Free" (BOGOF), or "Two for the Price of One."

The latter three can be especially useful to retain or increase sales yet still protect the underlying pricing and could help maintain or obtain suppliers' volume turnover discounts.

"Skimming" is another common technique, which you can use as a first-to-market tactic to recover research & development investment before the competition catches up.

"Penetration" pricing is a temporary, aggressive, targeted pricing tool to try to seize market share.

SHOE STORY

Quite regularly, Tina goes shopping for shoes. I have learnt to welcome her return and choice of new attire. So much so that I have discovered phrases, like "kitten heels, Roman ties and peep toes."

Almost every shoe ever made has a little sticker underneath that shows the price.

After she has told me how much she has saved me on the trip, I pluck up the courage to enquire about the cost. £29.00 is the proud response.

I glance at the sticker, which says £29.99 and say, "It states £30.00 here, so you have got even more of a bargain!"

"No, I paid £29.00," she argues.

"Well, no, I think you need to check the receipt," I joke.

Perception, psychological or last digit removal pricing is widely used and is popularly called "odd-value" pricing. It gives the impression of a cheaper price band, i.e., £14.99 instead of £15.00, £5,995 in place of £6,000 or, £99,999 to replace £100,000, etc.

CHAPTER FOURTEEN

BOOK & RECORD KEEPING

Do you need an accountant or book-keeper?

In the early stages, it is vital to understand where you are up to with money. There is no point waiting until the end of the year, middle of next month or even the end of this month, to find out your money in and money out status.

Try to get into the habit of doing your book-keeping every day.

There are many bespoke software systems, like Sage, Quick Books or you can buy pre-sectioned books from online retailers or stores such as WH Smiths. You can develop your reports with programs, like MS Word or Excel, while others may prefer hand-written information.

Crucially, do you understand the system you have chosen and can you spot errors when they occur or see when figures do not look right?

These days, many accountants prefer you to undertake book-keeping to keep their work-load down and simplify year-end paperwork.

Try to invoice promptly. Don't wait until the weekend because you are tired or too busy as you are giving your customer extra credit and running unnecessary risks with negative cashflow.

If we remember, it is cashflow, not lack of hard work, that kills off most start-ups.

Should you feel that you must have an accountant or book-keeper, ask around, take up references, inspect qualifications, indemnity insurance certificates and memberships of professional bodies. You may need to turn to in the event of a dispute.

Generally, book-keepers are cheaper than accountants. Many will visit you regularly, which is especially beneficial if you have payroll, VAT or foreign currency transactions.

However, the most crucial aspect is to find out what exactly you are getting and for what you are paying. Some accountants charge by the quarter-hour, even when there has only been one minute's phone conversation.

Can you ring to ask general questions or will you be charged? Does the service include final accounts? Will you be invoiced for time to discuss your affairs with the taxman? Will the services include your tax return?

There is much current focus on "the cloud." Can you speak to a real person if necessary and is there a cost? Who controls the password or software?

There are notable cases of individuals finding themselves in dispute and finding passwords no longer work. Then, they have no access to their invoicing, banking and other accounting information.

PROFIT AND LOSS

It is not the intention of this book to go into detail when it comes to accountancy, as this is substantially covered elsewhere. You can find some examples in the appendices.

However, in the early stages, simple Money In – Money Out records that will cascade into your Profit & Loss Forecasts and Statements are an excellent way forward. You can use bespoke software programs or hand-written or electronic methods.

The vital aspect is to ensure that you can spot errors and inaccuracies yourself and do not rely on automatically produced data that you just take for granted.

Another key is to stay on top of paperwork. Develop a "do it now" approach instead of leaving things to the end of the week or, worse still, month.

DEPRECIATION & CAPITAL ALLOWANCES

These are areas of which it is useful to have a basic understanding.

You can write down or write off assets in the books relevant to their useful working life.

Most tax authorities have rules by which you can spread the cost of a vehicle over a given period (often four years) to avoid a full expense in the year of purchase.

The accountancy term is depreciation, which tax authorities decline to recognise for tax purposes. Instead, many permit "capital allowances."

INCOME TAX & NATIONAL INSURANCE

It is essential to be able to assess what you may have to pay in Income Tax and National Insurance.

When will you have to pay it so that you can make appropriate provision for the charges?

There may be Payment on Account requirements based on previous year results.

Information is available on official government department websites, such as treasury, HMRC and leading accountancy firms.

Check that you are using the correct year as these allowances and tax rates can change annually.

It is also worth establishing when it comes to companies what if any, directors' benefits in kind charges might be applicable and what are the rules shareholders taking dividends.

In some cases, to stimulate growth and start-ups, governments may offer temporary national insurance or business rates holidays. The former does usually apply to directors.

VALUE ADDED TAX (VAT)

Another consideration is whether it is worth voluntarily registering for Value Added Tax, or if you must register for VAT compulsorily.

Check the current VAT threshold, different VAT rates and the various schemes available, such as fixed-rate, low turnover, cash and annual reporting.

HMRC's website explains how to register and make quarterly returns.

There are complex rules for the supply of foodstuffs, international transactions and second-hand goods. It is advisable to seek HMRC advice before commencing trading.

Importantly, if you are part of the VAT system, you will have to charge your customers VAT.

Are they VAT registered themselves or are they private individuals?

If you have voluntarily registered and many of your competitors have not, you may well have just become up to 20% more expensive!

There is a requirement to retain original records for six years.

An example of a VAT invoice is available in Appendix 5.

CHAPTER FIFTEEN

INTRODUCTION TO CASHFLOW

When producing a draft cashflow for the first time, it can be very daunting as you will have to make numerous assumptions (write these down). You will get better as you become more experienced and have real figures.

It is the most challenging task but arguably the most important and it is probably best left until last.

As we have said several times before, cashflow issues are the leading cause of start-up and general business failures. It is often the case when the order book is full, profits are satisfactory and when trying to expand.

It can be due to bad debt, slow payers or not having rapid access to sufficient working capital.

A crucial factor when considering the impact of cashflow is to make sure that you have allowed for the unexpected, i.e., order flow delays, payment delays, equipment breakdowns, etc. A rule of thumb is to establish all of your known costs and then add 30% as a contingency.

It is vital to have rapid access to cash and worth making sure that you have this available promptly well before you might need it in an emergency. When an event happens, it might well be too late!

If drafting a cashflow forecast for the first time, try to be cautious and pessimistic with sales and have robust contingencies when it comes to costs.

It is particularly important when calculating sales forecast income that it is not the date of sales that count but the time of payment.

When making a cashflow forecast, it is useful to separate the different elements. Split your fixed costs, rent, insurance, and rates etc., first. You have to pay these whatever happens.

Next, calculate the costs of making the actual sale, including materials or components.

Lastly, assess your general operating expenses.

A rule of thumb is to keep it simple. Don't go into the ninth degree. What you are trying to identify is the amount of money you will need above your expected spending for "working capital" to keep your business alive and functioning.

Some people call this the "POT" needed for the rainy day. It is much more than that as it is the life-blood of the business. It smooths income and expenditure to ensure you can pay bills and buy new stock.

You can find a partial cashflow forecast example in Appendix 6:

CHAPTER SIXTEEN

FINAL WORDS

Please remember that there are legal requirements for retaining and storing paperwork.

Vitally, you should install, apply and update regularly all security software like anti-virus and spyware detection.

Take regular backups and save them in a separate, secure location.

Good Luck!!!

SWOT

STRENGTHS	WEAKNESSES
High profile, modern location Previous sector experience & expertise Up to date qualifications and standards Knowledge of local market conditions Solid number of personal contacts	Challenges related to start-up Sole trader status Potential loss of key specialist personnel Present cashflow position No current formal backup support
OPPORTUNITIES	THREATS
Brand & reputation development Improved performance Global sector growth Achievement of work-life balance Social media leads & referrals	New and emerging sector competition Government policy Reputational risk Global economic conditions Professional indemnity claims

APPENDIX 2

LIFE CHANGING EXPERIENCES

Responsibility	Holidays
Control	Lifestyle
Long hours	Pension
Stress	No paid holidays
Illness	Reduced living standards
Job security	Transport
Family	Working conditions
Friends	

APPENDIX 3

PERSONAL SURVIVAL PLAN

	AMOUNT
ANNUAL INCOME	
Drawings or Salary from business	
Any Other Income	
TOTAL	
ANNUAL EXPENDITURE	
Mortgage or Rent	
General & Water Rates	
Property Insurance	
Gas, Electricity, Coal, Oil	
Personal Insurance	
Food & Household Expenses	
Clothing	
Telephone	
Hire Charges (TV, Video, etc.)	
Entertainment (Meals & Drinks)	
Subscriptions and Newspapers	
Car Tax, Insurance and Maintenance	
National Insurance Contributions	
Family Members' Expenditure & Presents	
Savings Plan	
HP and Loan Payments	
Christmas	
Holidays	
TOTAL	
NET TOTAL (Income less expenditure)	

APPENDIX 4

COMPETITOR COMPARISON

	OWN BUSINESS	COMPETITOR 1	COMPETITOR 2
PRICE			
CUSTOMERS			
REPUTATION			
QUALITY			
AVAILABILITY			
DELIVERY			
PROMOTION			
STAFF SKILLS			
LOCATION			
INCENTIVES			
AFTER-SALES SERVICE			

APPENDIX 5

INVOICE TEMPLATE

INVOICE

YOUR COMPANY NAME
YOUR ADDRESS

YOUR CONTACT DETAILS

DATE

CUSTOMER NAME
CUSTOMER ADDRESS

Order No.	Invoice No.	Description	Quantity	Price	Total
				Invoice Net	
				VAT @ x%	
				Invoice Total	

Payment Terms: strictly net thirty days.

Interest at 2% above XYZ Bank's Minimum Lending Rate will be applied to all overdue invoices.
BACS PAYMENTS CAN BE MADE TO THE FOLLOWING:
SORT CODE: XX-XX-XX
ACCOUNT NO: XXXXXX
Please reference payment with the above invoice number.

VAT REGISTRATION NO: XXXXX XXXX X

APPENDIX 6

CASHFLOW EXAMPLE

	Pre-start	1	2	3	4	5
OPENING BALANCE	0	1000	920	1100	1560	1990
INCOME						
Sales		0	300	600	600	800
Capital						
Loans & Grants						
TOTAL	**0**	**0**	**300**	**600**	**600**	**800**
EXPENDITURE						
Materials		50	50	70	120	200
Employ. Wages						
Income Tax/NI						
Rent & Rates		30	30	30	30	30
Heat & Light				20	20	20
Insurance						
Vehicle						
Telephone				20		
Advertising			40			
Bank Charges						
Sundry						
Cap. Exp.	135					
TOTAL	**135**	**80**	**120**	**140**	**170**	**250**
NET PROFIT/LOSS	**-135**	**-80**	**180**	**460**	**430**	**550**
- Personal Drawings	0	0	0	0	0	0
CLOSING BALANCE	**-135**	**920**	**1100**	**1560**	**1990**	**2540**

APPENDIX 7

CHECKLISTS

INSURANCE	LEGAL ISSUES
Business interruption	Advertising
Combined Policy	Agreements and contracts
Contents	Business insurance
Contract	Business status
Credit	Confusing names
Critical Illness	Data Protection
Employer's Liability	Debt control
Engineering Equipment	Employment
Fire and Other Hazards	Environmental
Goods in Transit	Finance
Health	Health & Safety
Income Protection	Intellectual property
Legal Expenses	Leases
Legal Protection	Planning Permission
Life	Refunds and returns
Mortgage or Loan repayment	Taxation
Key Person	Trading insolvently
National	Trading restrictions
Political Risk	Working from home
Premises	
Product Liability	
Professional Indemnity	
Public Liability	
Redundancy	
Repatriation	
Stock/inventory	
Tenancy	
Theft	
Travel	
Vehicle	

RECORDS	BUSINESS PLAN
Accounts	**Executive Summary**
Agreements, contracts	
Attendance	**Background**
Bank statements	Aim
Client, customer	Personal, Financial & Business Objectives
Company Register	Mission Statement
Competitors	Founders
Contacts	Advisors
Correspondence	Legal Structure
Data Protection	
Deeds	**Product or Service**
Disciplinary	Description
Employee	Pricing
Equipment, capital	Competition
Guarantees	Competitive Advantage
Health & Safety	
Holiday List	**Marketing**
Insurance	Target market
Invoices	Promotion
Licences	Sales Forecast
Maintenance	Risk & Threats
Manuals	
Mileage	**Operations**
Minutes	Process
Patents, copyright, trademarks	Distribution
Policies & Procedures	Suppliers
Price List	Employees
Professional advice	Premises
Qualifications, accreditations	Equipment
Quotes, estimates	
Receipts	**Finance**
Reconciliations	Setting Up Costs
Remittances	Break-even Analysis
Shares	Cashflow Forecast
Statements	Profit & Loss Forecast
Stock	
Suppliers	
Tax, NI	
Telephone	
Treatment	
VAT Returns	

APPENDIX 8

BUSINESS PLAN

Here is an example business plan to give you a feel for the level of detail you might need if approaching an investor or a bank:

ABC
25 West Street
Eastway
North Island

Business Plan

Tel:
Mob:
Email:
Web:

Prepared by:
Date:

Contents

1.0 Executive Summary

2.0 Background
2.1 Aim

2.2 Mission Statement

2.3 Founders

2.4 Advisors

2.5 Legal Structure

3.0 Product or Service
3.1 Description

3.2 Pricing

3.3 Competition

3.4 Competitive Advantage

4.0 Marketing
4.1 Target market

4.2 Promotion

4.3 Sales Forecast

4.4 Risk & Threats

5.0 Operations
5.1 Process

5.2 Distribution

5.3 Suppliers

5.4 Employees

5.5 Premises

5.6 Equipment

6.0 Finance
6.1 Setting Up Costs

6.2 Break-even Point

6.3 Cashflow Forecast

6.4 Profit & Loss Forecast

7.0 Appendices

7.1 CV

7.2 Competitor Comparison

7.3 Equipment List

7.4 Personal Survival Plan

1.0 Executive Summary

Our Company aims to sell widgets, which are a special version of the long-established product, to businesses and private individuals in North Island, at a profit. We plan to expand the business 10% per year and to export to the UK within three years.

We offer a specialised version of the widget for private individuals and organisations. Our version of the widget enables users to treble productivity because it uses our patented "E750" base material. E750 is only available from North Island and recent professional surveys show that supplies will last at least 100 years. ABC has secured a 10-year option on raw material

Founder and Managing Director Mr. Bob Quayle, who holds an MBA from the North Island International Business School. For fifteen years he was the Sales Manager of our main supplier and is the key person in the Company.

Mr. Jim Lowey is the company's technologist and manufacturer. He invented E750 and has more than 20 years of experience in the widget industry, having worked for two leading international manufacturers, BDC and BSS, in America.

The key strengths of the business are its innovative niche product, which offers a 300% improvement in efficiency and our employees, who have an outstanding track record.

ABC's main competitive advantage is its innovative product, which outperforms competitors' offerings. Mr. John Quayle, a nephew of the founder, has achieved the 2012 & 2013 "Widgetman of the Year" award from the industry's trade association.

Our target customers are in the West of the UK and near our location in Eastway.

We focus on customers that are under pressure by their customers to reduce cost and those who cannot afford to invest in expensive new machinery.

ABC predicts sales of Cream, Blue and Red widgets with installation and after-sales service will reach £350,000 next year.

2.0 Background

2.1 Aim

Our Company aims to sell widgets, which are a special version of the long-established product, to businesses and private individuals in North Island, at a profit. We plan to expand the business 10% per year and to export to the UK within three years.

We will break even in Year 2 and plan to improve our products every year.

We expect to achieve annual revenues of £500,000 by year 3.

Our main business objective is to provide a market-leading version of the widget within three years after launch at a gross profit of 60%.

The personal objectives of the founders are to be able to double their net disposable income and to become recognised by the business community as supplying the most cost-effective, high-quality widgets available.

2.2 Mission Statement

ABC aims to be the leading provider of specialised widgets to North Island and UK companies and private individuals by 2014. Our key focus is to deliver consistently high quality on time at a cost-effective price.

2.3 Founders

Mr. Bob Quayle is the founder and Managing Director. Miss Lisa Corrin acts as Company Secretary. The Sales Manager is Mrs. June Quayle.

2.4 Advisors

Accountants: Mr. James Kerruish of Kerruish & Co., Eastway, North Island.

Bankers: Mr. Paul Quilliam of the Island Bank Limited, Southway, North Island.

2.5 Legal Structure

The Company is a limited company. The registration number is 347628

3.0 Product/Service

3.1 Description

We offer a specialised version of the widget for private individuals and organisations. Our version of the widget enables users to treble productivity because it uses our patented "E750" base material. E750 is only available from North Island and recent professional surveys show that supplies will last at least 100 years.

We also provide installation, upgrading and full after-sales widget service.

3.2 Pricing

Our main product is the Cream Widget. The average sales price is £25 each

We also offer an installation service for £25 each.

Blue & Red widgets are also available at £45 and £15 respectively.

Servicing packs cost £100

3.3 Competition

Our main competitor on North Island is XWY. PRQ, a UK company, owns it.

In the UK, DEF and MNO are our biggest competitors.

These organisations control 75% of the known market and offer many other diverse products. They have operated for over fifty years.

We recognise that to take on XWY directly would not be sustainable and, consequently, we have developed a niche quality product, which outperforms existing competitive products by 300%.

Our product is more expensive than our competitors by 25%.

Rather than offer whole North Island and UK coverage, we focus on locations near Eastway and the West of the UK, where travel access is excellent.

3.4 Competitive Advantage

Our competitive advantage is our innovative product. It outperforms our competitors' offerings.

We have also secured an option of all of North Island's stock of E750 for the next ten years.

The excellent travel routes to the West of the UK allows target brief sales visits and, crucially, same-day delivery. Our investment in IT enables us to monitor our products at our main customers continually.

4.0 Marketing

4.1 Target Market

Our target customers are in the West of the UK and near our location in Eastway.

We focus on customers that are under pressure from their customers to reduce costs and those who cannot afford to invest in expensive new machinery.

Our product range is suitable for all widget buyers.

We aim at supplying smaller, flexible businesses. Usually, these have less than ten employees and turnover under £100,000.

Independent market research by IJH, available in Appendix 3, shows that there are 150 potential other customers.

4.2 Promotion

We access our customers through a combination of direct sales, third party distributors and our website.

Strategically, we have purchased advertising links on several trade association websites. We have carefully designed and taken specialist advice on the promotion of our website to search engines.

We recognise that website promotion and reliance on search engines will only generate about 20% of the sales required.

ABC has recruited one salesperson to directly sell to customers and provide after-sales service.

Though we advertise in some specialist trade publications, Yellow Pages and northisland.com, we have discovered that general-interest magazine and newspaper advertising is costly and ineffective.

ABC is proud to support the local community and sponsor Eastway Football Club. Several of its players work at our most significant local client.

We rely on word of mouth to generate 30% of existing sales. We are very conscious of the need to develop our reputation and react quickly to customer feedback.

Our promotion budget is £ 2,000 for the current year.

4.3 Sales Forecast
Predicted sales Year 1 are £350,000.

Cream Widgets
5,000 @ £25 each ex VAT = £125,000

Blue Widgets
2000 @£45 each ex VAT = £90,000

Red Widgets
1500 @ £15 each ex VAT = £22,500

Service, Installation
2250   @ £50 (average) =£112,500

4.4 Risk & Threats
The main threat to our business is increasing regulation, especially in the UK, which is placing increasing burdens on small businesses. It is

this artificial level playing field, which is forcing customers to source further and further afield.

Global competition remains a significant threat and manufacturing costs are under relentless pressure.

We are also aware of emerging competition from new manufacturers, which is the main reason for patenting E750 internationally. We know that there were risks in filing a public patent as it could be difficult to enforce against international manufacturers. Our existing customers have all signed confidentiality and exclusivity agreements.

5.0 Operations

5.1 Process
We take delivery of the base material for our widgets at our modern leased premises two miles from the mining company.

The raw materials are treated by heat and light to make E750. It is then moulded under pressure into widgets.

We have one modern production line supplied by RSU, the industry-standard manufacturer. We produce Cream widgets on Mondays, Thursdays and Fridays in a single 8-hour shift.

We make Blue widgets on Tuesdays and Red widgets on Wednesdays.

Customer servicing and installation are available daily on a call-out basis. When the team is not providing these activities, they carry out R&D and maintenance.

Finished products and raw material are stored separately to avoid cross-contamination. All waste is re-cycled in-house.

5.2 Distribution

Our main distribution channel is a dedicated courier service.

The specialist team handles servicing and installation.

Our UK distributors hold stock for direct delivery to their customers as well as providing larger sales orders for fulfilment from our factory. The dedicated courier service delivers products in the same way to direct customers.

5.3 Suppliers

We have an excellent relationship with our principal supplier, located two miles away, which has provided favourable terms of payment and stocking service. ABC has secured a 10-year purchase option on raw material supplies.

It is a very reputable company with a long track record, which has helped us develop E750.

The founder's father owns the business.

5.4 Employees

There are five employees in the business.

Founder and Managing Director, Mr. Bob Quayle holds an MBA from the North Island International Business School and for 15 years was the Sales Manager of our principal supplier.

He has five years of marketing experience from his role with LMN, a leading distributor of widgets.

Mrs. June Quayle, Sales Manager, was formerly Sales Director of our largest competitor, XWY. She worked there for twelve years before joining the company.

Miss Lisa Corrin, is a fully qualified accountant and has seven years' experience at the leading local practice, Kerruish & Co

Mr. Jim Lowey is the company's technologist and manufacturer. He invented E750 and has more than 20 years of experience in the Widget industry, having worked for two leading international manufacturers, BDC and BSS, in America.

Mr. John Quayle, a nephew of the founder, leads the production and distribution of widgets. Though he left school with no qualifications. John has established himself as a skilful producer of widgets and he received the prestigious 2007 & 2008 "Widgetman of the Year" awards from the industry's trade association for his achievements.

The annual employee account, including benefits, amounts to £80,000.

5.5 Premises
ABC's premises are located on an up and coming industrial estate to the North of the North Island's capital Eastway. We have a lease for 25 years and this renewable lease has 23 years to run. The annual charge is £5,000, with rent reviews every two years based on the UK Inflation Index. It consists of 20,000 sq. ft of production space with 2,000 sq. ft of office area.

Rates are payable at: £1,000 p.a.

Security devices protect the property and comprehensive insurance with EFG, under certificate number: 3311115544412, provides cover.

The leaseholder has agreed to modifications and planning permission has been granted.

5.6 Equipment

The Company owns the following equipment:

Item	Purpose	Purchase Date	Lifespan	Value
XXX	XXX	XXX	XXX	XXX
XXX	XXX	XXX	XXX	XXX
XXX	XXX	XXX	XXX	XXX
XXX	XXX	XXX	XXX	XXX
			Total:	

The Company will purchase the following equipment:

XXX	XXX	XXX	XXX	XXX
XXX	XXX	XXX	XXX	XXX
XXX	XXX	XXX	XXX	XXX
XXX	XXX	XXX	XXX	XXX
			Total:	

6.0 Financial

6.1 Setting-up Costs

£

Premises:
Refurbishment:
Equipment:
Vehicle:
Stock:
Insurance Premiums:
Professional Fees:
Stationery:
Other:

Total:

6.2 Break-even Point

6.3 Cashflow Forecast

6.4 Profit & Loss Forecast

7.0 Appendices

7.1 CV
7.2 Competitor Comparison
7.3 Equipment List
7.4 Personal Survival Plan

OTHER BOOKS BY THE AUTHOR

As Good As Gold - History of Pound Sterling. ISBN 0-9534818-4-0

De La Rue Straw Hats to Global Securities. ISBN 0- 9534818-2-4

Euro History & Development. ISBN 0-9534818-1-6

Holidays 2000 – A Time Capsule. ISBN 0-9534818-7-5

Negotiate to Win! - The Introductory Edition. ISBN 0-9534818-6-7

Start Any Business (eBook). ISBN 9781903467015

Scripophily - Historic Bond & Share Collecting. ISBN 0-9534818-5-9

The Eternal Old Lady - Bank of England. ISBN 0-9534818-3-2

The Hitmen - Part One. ISBN 0-9534818-8-3

FORTHCOMING BOOKS
BY THE AUTHOR

As Good As Gold (Print). ISBN 9781903467039
As Good As Gold (eBook). ISBN 9781903467121

Currants, Olives & Cotton (Print). ISBN 9781903467077
Currants, Olives & Cotton (eBook). ISBN 9781903467169

De La Rue (Print). ISBN 9781903467046
De La Rue (eBook). ISBN 9781903467138

Euro (Print). ISBN 9781903467053
Euro (eBook). ISBN 9781903467145

Scripophily (Print). ISBN 9781903467084
Scripophily (eBook). ISBN 9781903467176

Tail-less Cats & Three-legged Men (Print). ISBN 9781903467091
Tail-less Cats & Three-legged Men (eBook). ISBN 9781903467183

The Eternal Old Lady (Print). ISBN 9781903467060
The Eternal Old Lady (eBook). ISBN 9781903467152

The Green Shoots of Money (Print). ISBN 9781903467107
The Green Shoots of Money (eBook). ISBN 9781903467114

ABOUT THE AUTHOR

Ian Moncrief-Scott has over fifty years of broad business experience, mostly gained at international level, based in the UK.

As a former senior executive for a global publishing and information technology company headquartered in the USA, he has contributed to numerous client-facing procurement and outsourcing initiatives worldwide.

Ian has created and participated in numerous small businesses in the UK, Isle of Man and elsewhere.

He has also represented the Isle of Man Government Department for Enterprise in several of its business support schemes.

Ian designed and delivered extensive training for its Micro Business Grant Scheme.

In recognition of his long-term service to the Department, Ian was nominated for The Queen's Award for Enterprise Promotion and awarded an official Certificate of Recognition in 2018.